D1535216

SID STEPHEN

BEOTHUCK POEMS

AN OBERON BOOK

For Stephen Scobie

<u>auch - mud - yim.</u>
The Black man, or Red Indian's Devil
short & very thick ; He dresses in
Beaver Skin,
has a large beard &c.

<u>Seen at
the great
lake</u>

<u>a - ā - duth.</u> or Spear for killing Seals 12 feet long

bone
iron

amina   Deer Spear

iron

HISTORICAL NOTE

The Beothucks were the native inhabitants of Newfoundland when the first European fishing boats began to appear off the coast of the island in the mid-1400s. They lived a nomadic life, spending much of the year on the islands and arms of the east coast, and the winters inland, where the dense woods offered some protection against the harsh Atlantic storms. The Beothucks were a large people—some reports say that the men often exceeded six feet in height— but they seem to have lacked the aggressive nature of some North American tribes. They lived in extended families, and it is highly unlikely that they had any concept of the idea of private ownership except for small personal articles such as weapons and clothing.

They practised a form of sun worship, expressed in ritual having to do with fire and smoke. Red was considered a sacred colour, and they smeared the seams of their garments with red ochre, and used a mixture of ochre and grease on their bodies as well. This last led the early white explorers to call them "red indians," though in fact they were somewhat fair-skinned. They possessed no knowledge of metal work or ceramic art, but used stone or bark to make vessels and weapons. When worked metal became available, however, they showed themselves to be very adept at remanufacturing stolen or traded bits into hooks, arrowheads and other small tools.

There is some evidence to indicate that the first encounters between the whites and the Beothucks were peaceful; however these soon degenerated into quarrels over fishing sites and probably the natives' lack of an understanding of private ownership led to open hostility and finally complete distrust. Superior arms and aggressiveness made the conflict rather one-sided on the part of the whites, though there were isolated incidents in which the indians took the offensive and, when settlements began to be established on the coasts, the Beothucks were quite effective in terrorizing the small white population, particularly with their practice of removing the heads of their victims. Eventually, however, increasing pressure from the growing number of white settlements at prime fishing sites drove the Beothucks inland from the coasts, and the practice of open slaughter of indians by whites was joined to a policy of ignoring the situation by the government in St. John's. It appears that in a few generations the Beothucks lost the habit of their migratory lifecycle, and remained inland year round, never venturing to the sea-coast except in small food-gathering parties which were almost always immediately set upon by the whites, or by their allies the Mic-Mac indians from the maritime mainland, who had been brought to the island wholly for the purpose of hunting down the Beothucks.

By the year 1800, only a small number of the tribe remained alive, grouped in three or four family settlements on the shores of Red Indian Lake—now renamed Deer Lake—and near the headwaters of the Exploits River.

At this point the government of Newfoundland was prevailed upon to do something about the plight of the remaining Beothucks, who though for the most part sick and starving, were so afraid of the whites that they refused to be approached by anyone who tried to make contact with them. The Governor at St. John's offered a reward of about £100 to anyone who would bring in a living Beothuk: the idea was to befriend one and send him back to the tribe with offers of help and friendship, to lead the remaining indians out of the forests and into civilization. This plan was to seal the fate of the Beothucks, because while in the outports and settlements the indians were hunted almost as if for sport, *enough whites had sustained injuries while engaged in the practice that it was considered too dangerous to try to capture a male Beothuck. Thus a camp would be raided, and all the males and all but a few females would be killed immediately, in the hopes of capturing one or two females for the reward. Since the male members of the tribe traditionally sought the food and protected the females, this led to further deterioration of their condition.*

By the time the result of his policy was made known to the Governor, a few females had been captured but no contact had been made with the main remainder of the tribe, whose number had been decimated after five years of constant raiding and harassment. One woman taken in a raid was named Mary March—for the month of her capture— and had she not died before she could be returned to her people she might have been the key to survival for at least a few Beothuks. Another was Shawnadithit, who lived for some years after her capture with a man named John Peyton in a small coast settlement, and was taken to St. John's by the explorer and scholar William Cormack in 1827. She lived in his house there until her death in 1829, probably from consumption. She was buried in St. John's, but her grave has been lost to urban expansion. . . .

The few drawings and maps that Shawnadithit was able to make for Cormack, and the words of her language that she was able to teach him, are all that remain to link the Beothuck civilization with the one that wiped it out. These are retained in the Newfoundland Museum in St. John's, along with a collection of artifacts such as stone pots, pins made from bone and ivory and the exhumed remains of an adult and a child.

Sid Stephen
Shilo, Manitoba, 1976

LIFE/CYCLE

In the beginning
there was only the sea

or to be
      exact
there was the sea

      Island:
      changing sea sons
      carried seed-like
      in black boats circled
      through currents
            circled, settled here
      ringing the island
      as if it were a bell.

Sealskinned northern men
with ivory amulets

and norsemen losing spindle whorls
at l'Anse-aux-Meadows
looking for a land of vines
and finding
sea-scarred rocks and woods
as deep as the Atlantic.

Passing
like a thought
in a dream
in an instant: time
collects its wage of memory,
the tide breathes into
coves and rivermouths
and new life ripples over
rocks and sand. New men
who learn to use the land
in seasons,

moving from the seacoast
to the inland lakes each time
the leaves bleed on the trees,

who find within the earth
the ancient veins of ochre to protect
red veins within themselves,

who see the sun and stay
to hold the land as it becomes
a part of them   as they become

                "the people"
                Beothuk

I

"The Beothucks were found by the Cabots on their discovery of the island, and for nearly three and a half centuries continued to occupy this oldest British colony, living in primitive ignorance and barbarism, under our vaunted civilization, not altogether unknown, but unheeded and uncared for, until this same civilization blotted them out of existence"

—Howley, *The Red Indians of Newfoundland.*

SEAFIELD/HARVEST

Out of the sea
moving mind
on waves of smoke,
near water   trees

great grey fish
swim like thoughts,

becoming part
of the people,
holy   touched
with blood

       apart, touched

       not to be held

but kept in dreams   passing
in dreams of the people,
touched in songs and chants
   the seafields' shifting
rows of waves sucking
the rivers out of the land,

full of fish sent
arcing in half moons,

       alive, blood-
red as the earth
the water sunrise
red with blood and life.

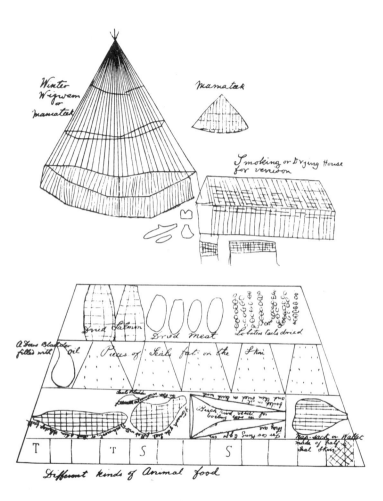

CEREMONY-THE PEOPLE GATHERED

The fire prepares the stones,
we push
the burning boughs away
and water is brought.

At a signal, rain
falls from our hands
in a thick arc

the stones split
to release clouds
to fill our bodies.
      Children are brought,
the old men heave
their heavy bodies
to breathe stoneclouds.

Just as the sun
falling each night into
the sea creates the clouds,
now we
create clouds, the sun colour
glowing through
the clouds

making us a part
of the sun.

BOATMAKER

Silently he bends white wood
near water,
wood becoming part of his red hands
as he has bent together
the canoe since daybreak,

without speaking: in his mind
            the new moon rides
            the river, ends upturned.
            This is
            the pattern, mind-held plan,
            the boat will be a child
            of the moon.

At night he eats in silence while
the moon drifts from its
sea-cave
to the riverbank,

is twinned
on the starry water.

On round riverstones
he sleeps, the moon/canoe
rising through his dream
full of fish
and the lives of hunters,

            the boatmaker
            hung between the points
            of the new moon.

movement of the trees
    wind within the mind
movement of the trees
    wind within the mind
movement of the trees
    wind within the mind
movement of the trees
    wind within the mind
movement of the trees
    wind within the mind
movement of the trees
    wind within the mind

    movement of the wind
        within the trees
        within the mind
            with   in

                the mind

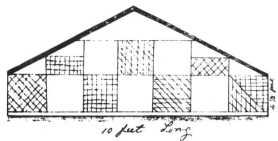

10 feet Long

Store House in which they put their dried venison,
in birch rind boxes or packages to keep during Winter

II

"We would have you inform yourself in the best manner you can. . . what course is best to be taken for planting of people in ye country, and for reducing the indians that live in New Found Land into civility, that they may be brot, in time, to know God"

—instructions to John Dowling, representative of the Council and Company of the New Found Land Plantation, 1640.

'ON FRIDAYS THE HOLY SHALL EAT ONLY THE FLESH OF FISH...'

And so the boats of other men
set out to net the oceans of the world
for the mouths
of Europe. It was
a question of salt,

of salt and the sun: the French
came salted within sight of
new-found land
and with fish for ballast
and profit
turned eastward
without ever keeling a beach.

But the dry English
came from an unleavened island,
knew commerce and sun
dried the fish gaping open
on beaches and stones,

and watched by people
who came from the forests
took sticks of pressed fish
to the wharves of Genoa and Naples
to feed the good Catholics.

The step between trust
and disaster
can't be seen
when it is taken, is only
visible
when viewed through the glass
of the future. A red hand

touched a white man's
hammer or awl,

the resulting blood
stains the roots of tolerance,
which die
and are washed out to sea.

NEW FOUND LANDFALL

Above the rotten canvas sails
the lookout
is half-mad with cold and thirst,
and there where waves run endlessly
he sees one wave
which does not run.

   Stars, followed by these men
   will never serve
   as their annunciation—
                         staggering ashore
wave-washed here
beached as whales
so long have they been in
another element,

they touch the land
at first
as they would touch a woman,

gently

and then as their strength
and confidence returns
they spread themselves upon it,
possessing it

pressing themselves into
the smooth bloodless beaches.

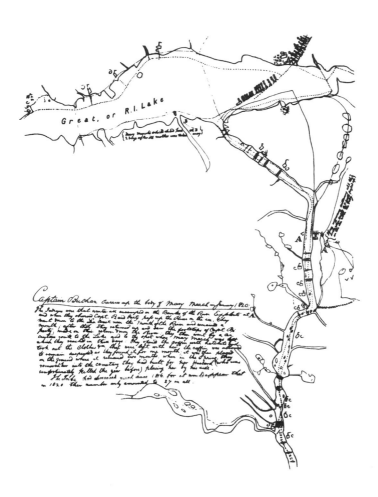

Great, or R.I. Lake

Captain Buchan came up the body of Mary March in January 1820.
The Indians were then encamped on the banks of the River Exploits at A
and when they observed Captn. B and party, kept up the River on the ice. They
went down to the sea coast near the mouth of the River and remained a
month, after that they returned up and saw the footsteps of Captn. B's
party, made on their return from the River, they then went by a circuitous
route to the lake and to the spot where Mary March's body lay,
when they reached in three days they opened the coffin with hatchets and
took out the clothes &c. that were left with her; the coffin was allowed
to remain suspended as they found it for one month, it was then placed
on the ground where it remained two months, when in the spring they
removed her into the cemetery they had built for her friends that was
unfortunately killed the year before, placing her by his side.
    The tribe had decreased much since 1816 for it was discovered that
in 1820 their number only amounted to 27 in all.

WHITE SETTLEMENTS

Between the forest
and the other dark lost land
of the sea

the first white settlers
hang
like bits of wax
on candle rims,

indefinite, undefined
by streets or schools,
melting at the back doors
into the great flame-like
heart
of this island. The sudden

warmth of cobwebs
on the face at night,
infernoes of indians
flicker in the trees
as easily as water flows
among the strange grey rocks.

Alone, unknowing: cold sparks
of fear of sickness, injury, of
indians and thunderstorms,
of madness and devils and the
dark endless woods

are struck
in dry white minds to feed
communities of panic,

the paranoia of
civilization
becomes rooted in the land

like a myth.

HISTORY

The heads are on poles
at the edge of the clearing.

We tell the story—the poles
are stained with the sun
colour, running from severed
necks.

We struck with stones and
bones broke apart, struck
down the guarding pale men,
we went forward over
their still bodies.

We tell the story—we
divide them at the neck,
the blood sun-coloured
runs back
is drunk by the earth,
at night the heads are raised up.

We turn the eyes to watch
the sun appear
out of the stomach of the sea.

We tell the story—the heads
are on poles
at the edge of the clearing.

drawn by Shanawdithit

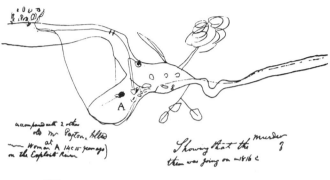

"いひひい
"いいひの

A

accompanied with 2 other
do Mr Peyton, killed
at A   14 c 15 years ago)
Woman at A   14 c 15 years ago)
on the Exploits River

Showing that the murder of
them was going on in 1816 c

1829

BETWEEN DEER FENCES

Starving is
dying is
measured in small noises
children make, in the pain
of empty breasts.

The long white night
of winter is spent beneath
the dry boughs
of an ancient deer fence.

Each motion brings dead flesh
painfully to life, brings
a silent shower of pine needles
to filter into patterns on the worn snow.

(Remember
animals running
fat with meat and terror
running between the broken trees
to where the hunters waited
near the river)

More snow, cold glory of
ice crystals
glaze the branches. In the morning
the woods
gleam
with death, a child dies.

In the morning
the people move toward the river,
scarring the new snow between
deer fences, coming to the river
through a swaying forest
of hard brilliant trees
weighed down with
shining antlers of ice.

Just before the shot
she turns and opens
the first furred red-seamed skin she wears,
exposing her self
skin smooth and hairless.

Her breasts are poles,
alpha/omega   are   hemispheres
of milk-filled flesh,
they pull the cursing hunter
to begin to end all things
between them,
generating guilt and lust
the heart pumping magnet draws
the white face closer,

(in an instant she becomes
a compass followed
to its own
spinning conclusion,
a lodestone in the forest
for these men

who finally mis-read the gesture
turn and aim their power
at the one who stands between them,
in a flash of
gunpowder
bring down the man whose child
has filled her breasts with milk.

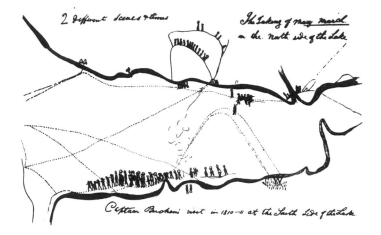

2 different scenes & times

The taking of mary march
on the north side of the lake

Captain Buchan's visit in 1810-11 at the South side of the Lake

MARY MARCH 2

After the long winter
among the white

promises, they brought her back
to her people
like a bribe.

Filled with
tuberculosis
she had learned
in St. John's,
she must have known
how to die

quietly letting go
of life

on board a ship
two days away
from the shore
of her people's graves.

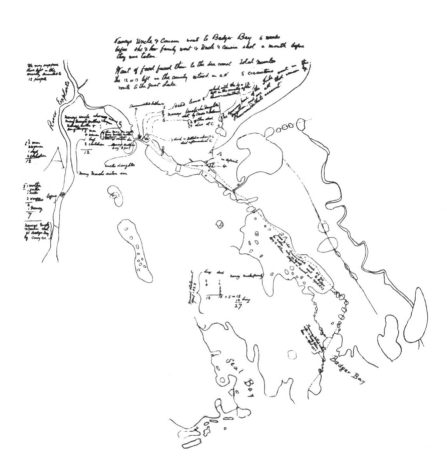

III

"There is a great difference in the quality of workmanship of various examples of each type. The higher quality specimens on the left of each group may be regarded as the type of specimens from the time when the Beothuks were rich and prosperous. The more degenerate specimens were probably made later when the tribe were living a hand to mouth existence shortly before their extermination"

—card on a display case containing Beothuk artifacts in the Newfoundland Museum, St. John's, Newfoundland.

SHAWNADITHIT

The meaning of the name
is   lost
is   in the sound
      the shift
      and fall of
      water
      on stone steps
      there
is   something of
a going-out of fires,

the finality of languages
forgotten
in the parting syllable.

True history: is what lives
                 within the mind,
                 is
                 of the tongue,
                 is
                 seen by the mind's I,

                 does not die with language, lives
                 in the sound of words
                 whose meaning
                 is forgotten.

SHE IS WOUNDED IN A RAID

    The arcs of flesh and fire
intersect,
her hand becomes her self: all

the slow identifying whorls
fill with her blood,
a space appears where just a

pulse ago was
stretched skin, tight as moss
across a stone/hand.

    She looks through her hand.
The grass moves beneath her,
the secret framework
of her body shivering
without its covering
of human leather,

          then turns to run,
          folding up her hand full
          of holes, which later sealed
          themselves into
          white stars,

          she holds a galaxy of pain
          between her breasts,

her severed life-line
bracketing the wound.

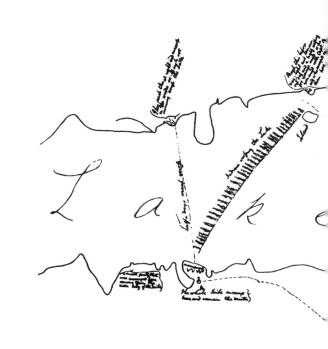

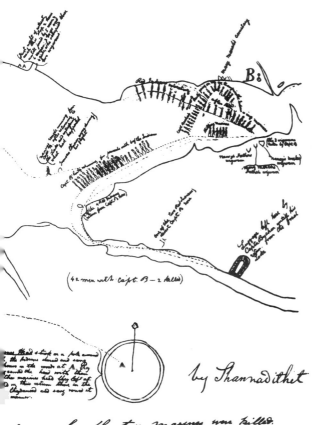

(42 men with Capt. B — 2 killed)

by Shannadithet

1810-11 when the two marines were killed.

SHE DRAWS A DEER
FOR MR. CORMACK

The living pen
fifth finger held
among the other four spills
a perfect deer

on the white paper,

touched exactly
as a bird alighting
on a maple branch: she draws

from memory

tail
hindquarters
underbelly, front legs
stiff and smooth,
tilted head, the back
a bridge arc'd from
the antlers to the

tail again, the deer flows
from her memory, remembering
the deer in danger

held now in ink.

OTHER DRAWINGS
FROM ST. JOHN'S

        Thin glass breaks
the light above the desk
where Shawnadithit draws
her stories with her starred hand,
red ink for her people
and the curving lines of lakeshore
and the white men done in black.

        "Here Mr. Peyton shot
        a woman. . . here
        we placed two heads
        on poles and danced around"

        Cormack writes her words
in symbols she cannot
understand: the drawings speak
for her, his English words
interfere with her forest.

        "Here we were hungry. . . this
        is where my father and his
        brother went for food, they were
        shot here"

        Again the words are written,
she takes the pen again
but now
Cormack sees that she is drawing
with her lungs: bright bits of
blood appear
to mark her own redness
on her handkerchief,

on the paper other indians
are drawn in red.

The House in St John's in which Shawnawdithit lived (Roopes) drawn by herself.

SHE ATTENDS CHURCH
WITH THE CORMACKS

      Atop the history of her own
dead people, the triumph of a
civilization washed ashore
three hundred years ago: she kneels

when the Cormack family kneels,
stands erect in her cast-off clothes
and hears God's servant call on God
to witness her salvation.

      The plaster son upon the cross
      has wounded hands, she sees
      the painted blood
      clotted on his fastened limbs.
       Her own hands
      meeting one another in the darkness
      of her folded coat
      feel warm,
      the right explores the scars upon
      the left.

She leaves the church her body,
she leaves the church
and sees her child's dead father
at the ceremony of the stones,
he breathes the heavy vapour standing
in his reddened deerskins
with his hand upon her own, unbroken skin.

    Her tears pass for a blessing.
    It is time to leave the church,
    return
    to the cold frustration
    of her room
    in the stone house above the harbour.

SHE SAYS GOODBYE
TO MR. CORMACK

So much is left unsaid: words
leave so little
to the imagination,

the white explorer
who brought his
English questions to the island,

and now is leaving
for another coast.

A round grey stone
is placed between them
in the room. Light reflects
where words
echo without meaning.

(The stone is from
her lakeshore: her tongue
is even now becoming
stone,
dense with silence
and hard with meaning,

a crystal fragment
held within her mouth.)

The stone on the table
creates its own space,
is
self-defining: there are
none like it anywhere.

She lifts the stone
and passes it to him. It is

as heavy as the words for

goodbye

final

done.

SHE DIES IN ST. JOHN'S

June 6, 1829:   the morning
when the self-willed wind
hung silent in the branches

of her ruined lungs. Outside
the streets are filled
with early-morning fog,

(not present on her face
reflected in her bed,
but here the sea-mist
curls upon itself,
in the absence of the wind).

Her body stiffens
stripped of life
as a tree is stripped by fire,
creating the draught
in which it is consumed
by the very truth
of its burning.

The fog is stained red
as the sun rises through it,
is burned off, disappears

the arc of her people
ends
in a small stone house
above the harbour.

As temporary as a rainbow,
not replaced but taken by the earth,
changed and unchanged,
the story
becomes the land,
the teller becomes
what is told.

She will be buried
in the great vault of this island,

the story will be whispered
but not told.

   (Stop short of pity. Don't
   mythologize
   the Cain in every one of us.

   Graves outlive
   all our other monuments
   because
   they represent
   more guilt than pride.

   Her space inside the earth
   will be lost,
   will be found to be
   all
   there is to be.

IV

"Welcome to Newfoundland—

Britain's oldest colony,
Canada's youngest Province"

 —sign on highway at Port-aux-Basques, Newfoundland.

FIRST IMPRESSION

The nightboat slipped
into its element, moved
snail-slow on a trail
of its own spit,

the salt air cured
my sleeplessness

though all night long
the island glowed inside
my radar mind, goldringed
like a bride.

At five AM on the
line between the sky and sea is

land, the first notes
of a seaborne foghorn mourn
the coming of the nightboat.

Finally, consumed by morning
the nightboat leans against the pier
at Port-aux-Basques
and rests while I go on,

breaking the highway silence,
entering the inside of the island
like a lover.

BUS STATION

It's noon, it's like
a western movie: there's
a dusty silence here,
I walk up to the counter with my bill

and my beard and lack of accent
(left behind me years ago)
betray me.

A voice asks "What are those?"

(I hear myself)

and watch a card of key-chains
stop before me. They are
made in Taiwan, show
plastic indians about to shoot
a bow.

The voice says "How is that pronounced?"

The girl says "Be–o–tuk I guess"

and so I pay my bill and for a dollar
buy a key-ring.

> The silence continues
> as I leave the lunch counter,
> walk up to the intersection.
>
> The leaves have turned
> their backs on summer.

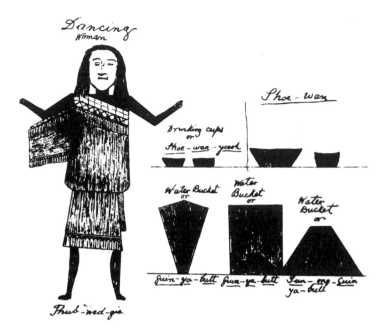

Dancing
Woman

Phub - ned - gie.

Shoe - wan

Drinking cups
or
Shoe - wan - yeesh

Water Bucket
or
Quin - ya - butt

Water
Bucket
or
Quin - ya - butt

Water
Bucket
or
Sun - ong - Quin
ya - butt

BEOTHUCK CHILD:
NEWFOUNDLAND MUSEUM

No pile of stones
within the earth,
his grave is bright
-ly lit
and in it he
hangs sideways,
a human bat wrapt
in his coat
of skin.

His skull gleams
with knowledge
held forever: in
the dried
streams
of his mind   the fish
still swim
he stoops to pick
red berries, holds
the red-stained doll
which lies beside him now.

(At night he spreads
his shoulder's blades
swims in the memories
which radiate
from his closed eyes—
    that is why he smiles,
    his lips drawn back
    full of power and the spirit
    moving)

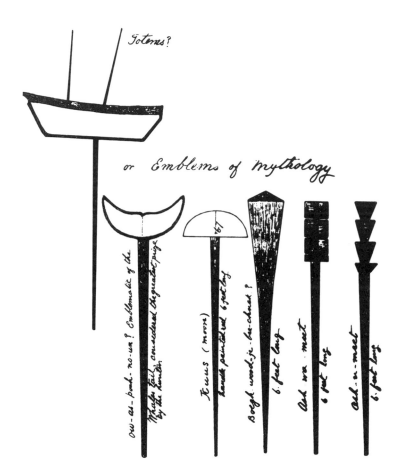

Totems?

or Emblems of Mythology

Ow-ai-bud. no-un? Emblematic of the
Whale Tail. considered the greatest prize
by the Hunters.

Kuus (moon)
heads painted red 6 feet long.

Doogl wood-je- he-chnut ?
6 feet long

Ah-wa-met
6 feet long

Ah-a-met
6 feet long

BONE PINS

Gripped in tight white light
are splinters of ivory, bits of bone,
they shimmer   at the bottom of the case,
swimming in light.

> Here I am
> looking for patterns, proof
> of evolution
> in these incised plates: clothespins

come to mind,
the old kind which are
knob-headed, split

but these clothespins are
flat, traced with thoughts
which change with every red
filled line,
they lie splayed apart
in this harsh museum morning.

Listen: here
is the click and shift of years,
the pins
lifting/falling on leather thongs,
dancing

as leaves on trees
dance in the winds
and fall

into the cold autumn bonfire
of this room.

BUMPER STICKER

A Cadillac
wears an orange and blue
Conservative
bumper sticker,

election is today. On Water Street
the driver parks the car,
asks me to change
a quarter for him.

I had no change,
though his lapel pin told me
that it was time for one.

   (Things have changed already,
   in the forest mines tunnel
   through the graves
   of the Beothucks,
   not even the children
   are safe now,

   the Newfie Bullet used to pass
   through Exploits, now
   the Greyhound Buses
   have replaced the train
   which has replaced
   the trails,

the only living father
of Confederation
stares through the fog
at the oil refinery and wonders
if the people will
"trust Joey"
one more time.)

Change? Who would Shawnadithit
vote for?
            and he laughs: explains,
                              he's from Toronto,

just another in an ancient line
who washed ashore on this
New Found Land.

From the beginning
is land
was land taken
from the sea: strong, rock

solid, yet it was
the stone which gave in
to the sea. All
that land can do
is to surrender in degrees,

save here a streaked
promontory
there a single pinnacle

finally no more than
a mother of currents,

ripplemaker

hoarding the ebbed hours
of the sun.

No more than this: it is men
who place an

I

in island.

Copyright © 1976 by Sid Stephen

The drawings by Shawnadithit are reproduced by permission from the originals in the Newfoundland Museum.

ISBN 0 88750 121 4 (hardcover)
ISBN 0 88750 162 1 (softcover)

Editor: Gail Low

Printed in Canada

PUBLISHED IN CANADA BY OBERON PRESS